How To Get
Any Project Done In
Just 2 Hours Per Day

- By Jim Edwards

How To Get Any Project Done In Just 2 Hours Per Day

Published by **AQuickReadBook**.com™
A Division of Guaranteed Response Marketing, LLC

A Quick Read Book™ is a Trademark of Guaranteed Response Marketing, LLC

Printed in the United States of America
ISBN: 1452870063

For Terri,
who always believed in me, even when I didn't.

For little Johnny,
who showed me the meaning of unconditional love.

For my parents, Pat & Dallas…
see, all that talking when I was a little kid
finally paid off!

WHAT IS A QUICK READ BOOK™?

A Quick Read Book™ helps authors and readers connect much faster than with a traditional book.

> **FACT**: We live in a fast-paced, "need-it-now" society.

> **FACT**: Traditional books contain 20% content, and 80% "extra" that just fills up pages to add "bulk".

> **FACT**: People don't have time to waste, especially when it comes to solving pressing issues and problems in their business or personal lives.

A Quick Read Book™ solves all those problems, and much, MUCH more!

As a reader, you get to cut straight to the heart of a book's contents, without wading through hundreds of extra pages of fluff. You get exactly what you need to succeed with the author's topic, and none of the extra filler.

As an author, you get to share the exact facts, tips, tricks and insider information your audience needs to succeed. And you don't have the pressure from a traditional publisher that just wants to fill pages with unnecessary text.

For more **A Quick Read Book**™ titles and information about becoming **A Quick Read Book**™ author, please visit us at the **www.AQuickReadBook.com**™ publisher's website today.

About Jim Edwards

Jim Edwards, founder of Guaranteed Response Marketing, LLC, is an Internet expert, marketing entrepreneur, newspaper columnist, author, motivational speaker and elite mentor and coach.

Having gained personal and financial freedom for himself and his family, he shares his proven strategies with self-motivated, hardworking people to help them attain personal and financial independence.

He has written and published dozens of ebooks, print books and hundreds of articles. Through his company, Jim has produced some 30 informational products on DVD and many more available in the latest electronic formats downloadable from the Internet. Jim produces and hosts webinars on a weekly basis and has been a frequent guest speaker at numerous international Internet marketing seminars.

He offers the exclusive "Jim Boat" seminar, an intensive seven-day program integrated into a Caribbean cruise, an inspirational setting for focusing on ways to achieve success. In its third year, the 2009 Jim Boat included over 100 participants from six countries.

Jim's successes are most compelling because they stem from his true life story. From childhood Jim was always driven to succeed. Though he excelled as a young man in real estate and mortgage banking, Jim left the industry to launch his own business.

In just a few short years, his business failed, he lost all he acquired, and he struggled to support his family and survive.

He developed a heart condition and landed in the hospital staring death in the face. Thereafter, he declared bankruptcy.

With only one way to go, Jim climbed his way up, up and up using his keen mastery of the Internet, a simple marketing strategy and hard, honest work.

Within two years he was financially stable and free.

A prolific creator and writer, Jim constantly has several books and new products in development at any given time.

What motivates him most is seeing how his work helps others free themselves of the shackles of financial servitude to the corporate world. His goal is to help self-motivated smart, hard-workers liberate themselves from the corporate establishment to build their own business and attain personal freedom.

He has been featured in Entrepreneur magazine, and his products have ranked number one best selling in the educational, business and economics and special interest, business categories on Amazon.

His latest works include *The Net Reporter*, *True Life Success Lessons* and the wildly successful *I Gotta Tell You* blog and newsletter.

Find out more about Jim's latest projects here:

Table of Contents

Introduction

Welcome, everybody. This is Jim Edwards and welcome back to another The Net Reporter Webinar. Tonight we have a great presentation on how to get any project done, in just 2 hours per day. These are my actual real strategies for ultimate productivity.

I just want to let you all know that we have lots to cover and you will probably want to watch this a couple times. So, of course, if you're watching this live, we'll have a replay for you, as well as a transcript and some other goodies coming out as a result of this.

I just want you to know that this is actually what I do and how I think and how I get stuff done. So if you've ever wondered how I'm able to get so much done, this is a scary peek inside Jim's brain to see how I think and what I do.

With no further ado, let's dive right in.

Here's what we're going to cover today. We're going to cover two paths for getting any project done; how I get it all done even when my time is crunched.

How to prioritize, which projects to work on first. Two types of planning, that is, strategic versus action planning. The Fast Action Matrix. Deadlines versus goals. This is one where I think I'm going to ruffle a few feathers, but as you know, I don't care.

I'm going to give you a tale of two builders. And we're going to do live Q&A about this session's topics. And, of course, the ubiquitous much, much more.

Audience Survey

First I want to do a quick audience survey. I just want to know who's here and how we're thinking. I had some people before we jumped on the Webinar and starting presenting, telling me that they really needed this and they were looking forward to it. So I just want to have an idea of who's out there.

We'll open this first poll. "Do you bust your butt but you don't seem to get any closer to your goals very fast?" Just choose one.

Your choices are yes, very much so, yes, sometimes I feel that way. Another one, not really. And then no, I'm right on target.

We've got about 50, 61% of the votes in, so we will… the quicker you vote right there on the screen and click the Submit button, the sooner we can keep moving on and get into the good information. But this really helps us all know who's here and where we are.

I'll do a little countdown. Five, four, three, two, one. Close the poll. Let's look at the results.

This is not surprising, but 26% say yes, very much so; 68% say yes, sometimes I feel that way; and 6% say, not really. That's interesting. That tells me that 94% of the people here feel like they're spinning their wheels.

Now I just want to do another quick audience poll. This one's a little bit of a different twist on the same question. This question is "Do you feel like you're spinning your wheels more than half the time you're working on your online business?" Your choices are yes, and I'd like to stop now; yes, but I'm making progress; or no, I'm pretty efficient when I work; or no, I'm always on target.

We've got about 67% of the votes in, 72. I need to get some better game show music than just me rattling on. 86% of the vote in, so we'll do a little countdown. Five, four, three, two, one.

Let's look at the results. 34% say yes, and I'd like to stop now. 59% yes, but I'm making progress. And 6% say they're pretty efficient when they work. So congratulations to you. But I guarantee you, even if you're in that 6% you're going to pick up some things

4

tonight that are going to help you be even more efficient. For the rest of you, I think you're going to get a lot of good insight.

Let's continue.

The Big Picture

Now let's take a look at the big picture of getting it all done, or actually getting any project done. And this is more like the satellite view. This is the view of any project that has to go through these steps that I'm going to show you right here. Anybody who successfully and basically does anything, especially a project, is going to have to do it this way to some degree.

The first thing you've got to do is know what you want to get done. You've got have some sort of a goal. It helps to be able to write that down and put it above your computer monitor. Then you can always take a peek back and say "Okay, this is what I'm supposed to be working on right now. This is the umbrella."

Next thing you got to know is why you're doing it. Because if you say "Well, I've got to… you know, I'm going to get an eBook and I'm going to get a website up. Oh I'm going to get one of these here online businesses set up"

Well, okay. But when you hit those roadblocks, it helps to know why you're doing it. And one of the more powerful why I've ever had, I needed to feed my family. I sure as hell didn't want to go down and get a job at Lowe's.

Now there's nothing wrong with working at Lowe's, but old Jimbo does not do too well with manual labor. So one of the most powerful ones was, I've got to pay the bills and I've got to save the money and I got to make it happen.

Then you need to plan out what needs to get done. And this is real simple. This is a list. This is not your final list, but you need to plan out what needs to get done.

Think in terms of action items, meaning what needs to get done; materials needed, i.e., what you're going to need to get it done. If you're building a fence you're going to need barbed wire or you're going to need wood. If you're building a website there are certain things you're going to need, like a domain name, hosting. And there are going to be certain costs associated with that.

You need to plan that out so you know, based on what you're trying to get done, how much you should expect to be able to pay. If it's more than you're able to pay, then you need to drop back, find a project you can take care of and you can accomplish.

I know that that may seem like common sense, but you'd be surprised how many people get started with a project. It doesn't get finished because they didn't sit down and figure out what needed to get done or what they would need or how much it was going to cost.

Then you need to decide who's going to do each item and when. And there're only two choices. Either you're going to do it or somebody else is going to do it. And there is no in-between. Now you can have software do it. But ultimately, even if software is accomplishing a task, somebody's got to set the software up. And then you take action.

Once you know what you want to get done, why you want to get it done, you plan now what needs to get done. You decide who's doing it, then you just need to take massive action until it's done.

I am going to get a little more in depth than this. But I just want to show you that no matter what you're doing, whether you're Bill Gates at Microsoft or whether you're Joe Blow figuring out delivering papers, you go through these steps whenever you're looking to accomplish basically anything.

These five keys apply to projects big and small. It doesn't matter what you're doing, how big the project is or small the project is, these are the steps that you go through.

Now, there are two paths for getting any project done. The question you need to ask is which path are you going to take? But first, I want to tell you a story. My youngsters, gather round to Uncle Jim and he's going to tell you a story, a tale of two builders. It was the best of times and it was the worst of times.

Now, a little background.

A Tale of 2 Builders

Terri and I are building two houses right now. We're actually building one new construction and we're almost tripling the square footage of another house. Let me tell you, building one house is stressful enough. But building two houses has damned near put me in the hospital. But, it's also been a great learning experience, because I've watched two builders with completely different styles. And it has brought home to me so much, the way that people work and how it impacts efficiency and impacts the time it takes to get a project done.

The first builder, Builder 1, does everything in order, one thing from the next. Not "one" thing from the next, but one thing from the next. That means that once one job is done, then he worries about the next job. And nothing gets ordered, no subcontractors get arranged for the next job, until each job is done.

So, the carpet wasn't even ordered until some other things got done ahead of time. We just got into a situation here which really pissed me off. The situation is that we have a shower, thank God, because I do bathe occasionally. And the shower is going to require a custom door, a custom glass door. Now we've known about this for months. And he comes to us two days ago and says, "Oh, we're getting on towards being done. And so y'all need to go down and pick out the shower door. It's going to take between 2 to 3 weeks to get it."

And I'm like uh, didn't we know that we'd need this now? Why is this just now being taken care of? Uh, I just didn't get around to it. If the specter of spending 30 years in prison wasn't enough to keep me from throttling this guy, I might be doing this broadcast from Rikers Island.

Anyway, this guy operates from a checklist and he's very, very methodical. Now his work is not bad. I mean, he does good work, quality work. But he operates from a checklist, a single linear checklist. And the problem is he often has huge delays in getting anything done. The house so far has taken 287 days,where we've been working on getting this house done. And the job was promised at 90 days.

Needless to say, this builder sucks in my opinion. This story is going somewhere, children, so just hang with me.

Builder No. 2 arranges to have multiple subcontractors working at the same time when possible. So there have been times when I've been out to the house and the plumber's been working inside, the concrete guy is outside working on the sidewalk, and the roofer is up there putting on the roof. And so he's got three different people working on three different things simultaneously.

He also plans ahead for when he'll need the next job done or the material delivered. For example, not too long ago all the siding was delivered on Friday and the man started putting on the siding on Monday. Because he knew the guy was going to be there to put the stuff on Monday, he had the siding delivered on Friday.

He also has backup plans.

Last week the electrician didn't show up, so he had another electrician that he knew he could call. And that person was there the very next day to get the job

13

done. So instead of waiting for the knucklehead, or having to figure out what to do, he had a contingency plan in place.

The result: The bigger house is going to be done in 130 days or less. This is actually a bigger house being built, plus an exterior detached 2-car garage with an apartment over the top of it. He's going to be done in less than half the time because he's organized.

I didn't really have a happy noise to go with the happy face, so I'll make a happy noise. Ahhhh.

Where is all this going? Well, this is a perfect illustration of the two ways and only two ways that you can do virtually any project. And what do I mean? Well, we're back to where we started: two paths for getting any project done. Which path are you going to take?

The Linear Model

The first path is the linear workflow. This is an example, a typical downloadable information product sold from a website. What you'll notice, this is pretty close to the linear way that you're taught to do this.

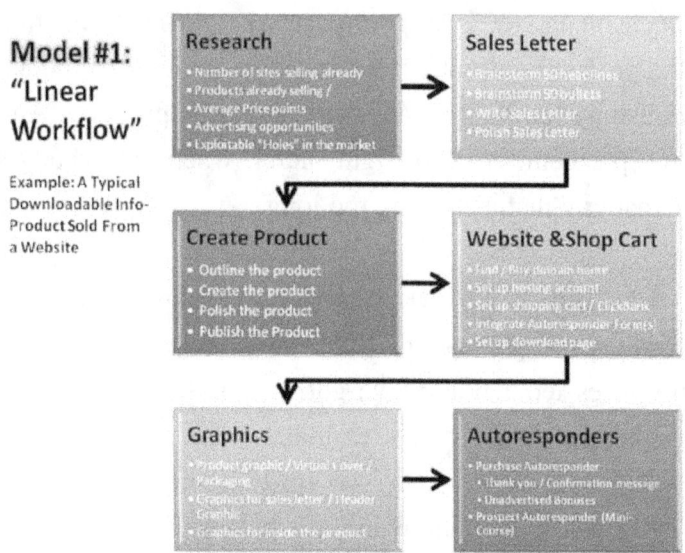

First you do your research. You go out and you look for sites, advertising opportunities and exploitable holes in the market. Then we move over to writing the sales letter.

I will tell you this fact from my own personal experience from having done some very, very high level coaching. When you're doing this yourself, when you get to this stage of the process, this is the No. 1 place where people bog down. Doing the headlines, doing the bullets, writing the sales letter and polishing the sales letter, is the No. 1 dropout point.

The No. 2 dropout point is right here, creating the product; outlining the product, creating the product, polishing the product and publishing the product. And the problem is also right here, when everybody's screaming that it's taking too long.

If you do make it over here, now people are freaking out because it's time to switch gears. I've got my sales letter done; I've got my product done. I've got to get that, I've got to make some money, got to make some money. So I've got to get my website up, got to get my domain name, my hosting account. How the hell do I do ClickBank? I've got to get the auto responder set up. Oh, and I've got to set up that down-load page.

Once they do make it past here, then they get their graphics. Oh, yeah, I've got to get one of them eBook covers and all that other stuff. Then finally they get their auto responder, messages and everything taken care of, and then we move on to traffic and ongoing business and things of that nature.

I want you to notice here, the way most people do it, is that nothing happens out of order. This is an exact, just change the things, the action items, but this is exactly how Builder No. 1 does it. And nobody wants to be like Builder No. 1. Especially if Jim's contemplating… I shouldn't say that in the recording … but Jim is not happy with Builder No. 1 in any way, shape or form.

This is a great example of the person that takes six months to try to get something done, just to get a simple eBook up for sale. They feel like they have to, A, do it in order; and B, they have to do it all them-selves. And C, they don't understand the different classifications of activity going on here as well as their own (I'm not going to say biorhythms), but their own way of operating. And they're not maximizing their time correctly. And that's where the two hours comes in. We're going to cover that in a minute.

There's a concept I want to get across to you and I hope that you write this down. All right? There's a difference between knowing what needs to be done and doing it yourself. Good example … the drywall in these two houses.

Builder No. 1 looked at me and said yes, we could hire a crew to do this and they'd be done in two to three days, but we're going to do it ourselves and we should be done in about a week. It took them 2-1/2 weeks to do the drywall.

Now he's told that he has an overhead each month of $10,000. That's what he's got to make to cover his nut.

The other builder hired a gang to come in and do it and they were done in 3 days. Now which of these do you think cost more to actually do that drywall job, the one that took 2-1/2 weeks or the one who did it in 3-1/2 days because he hired somebody else to do it? The guy it cost more is right here, because he spent the majority of that month doing one simple job, that this guy got done in 3 days.

18

Understand, especially with an online business, what people fall into. They're like okay, this is what needs to get done. So I need to figure out or I need to learn or I need to be the one who does it. That's not the case. You need to understand, and we're not going to get into this right now. But the bottom line, you have to understand what an hour of your time is worth. Okay? If you know what an hour of your time is worth, then you know whether you should be doing it or you should be outsourcing it.

It's fine to know what needs to get done and it's fine to do some of it. But you don't want to do all of it, because then you're going to be just like Builder No. 1.

I know that some people don't have a ton of money. "Jim, I'm not like you. I don't have hundred dollar bills falling out of my pockets walking down the street. I'm not rich like you." Well, gang, I ain't rich. And I don't have hundred dollar bills falling out of my pockets.

It's funny; I love the image I think some people have of me. But the bottom line is, if you can't hire somebody else to do it, then I'm about to show you a way that you can get it done. But I just want you to

19

understand something. If you make $1000 a week and you work 40 hours a week, that means you make $25 an hour.

You should not be doing anything that you can hire somebody else to do for less than $25 an hour, even if you can do it yourself. Because when I show you in just a sec, you're going to see how you can get stuff done a lot quicker.

Anyway, this is Model No. 1. This is the linear workflow. It's not a bad model; it's just not an efficient model. I will also tell you that I've used this model before. And only when I learned how to delegate and understood what I'm about to show you, then I was able to start doing what I call simultaneous workflow channels.

Simultaneous Workflow Channels

That may sound complicated, but it's not. And this is actually a great example of Builder No. 2 and how he works and how you should work when it comes to your online business.

Model #2:
"Simultaneous Workflow Channels"

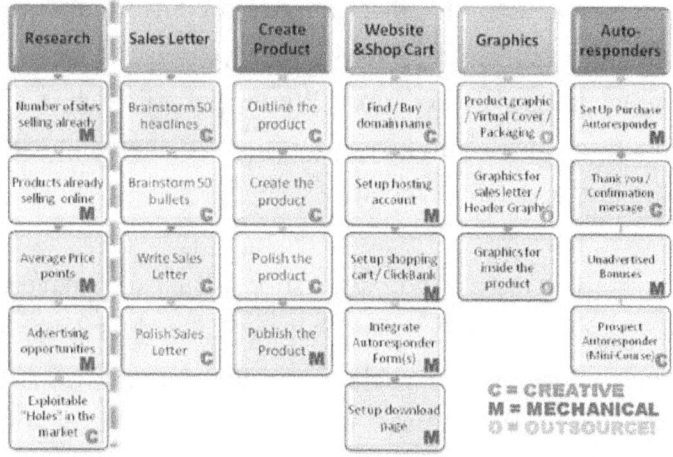

Research	Sales Letter	Create Product	Website &Shop Cart	Graphics	Auto-responders
Number of sites selling already M	Brainstorm 50 headlines C	Outline the product C	Find / Buy domain name C	Product graphic / Virtual Cover / Packaging O	Set Up Purchase Autoresponder M
Products already selling online M	Brainstorm 50 bullets C	Create the product C	Set up hosting account M	Graphics for sales letter / Header Graphic O	Thank you / Confirmation message C
Average Price points M	Write Sales Letter C	Polish the product C	Set up shopping cart / ClickBank M	Graphics for inside the product O	Unadvertised Bonuses M
Advertising opportunities M	Polish Sales Letter C	Publish the Product M	Integrate Autoresponder Form(s) M		Prospect Autoresponder (Mini-Course) C
Exploitable "Holes" in the market C			Set up download page M		

C = CREATIVE
M = MECHANICAL
O = OUTSOURCE!

To continue the online business example, we have here the same exact activities that were listed on the previous example. But instead of having one go to the next to the next to the next to the next, we can divide them up into groups. Then we see them as distinct subsets or groups of activity.

The first thing you're always going to want to do, and that's why there's a line here. The first thing you always want to do is your research. You want to know whether you should be getting into a market. You want to know whether there's an opportunity there and what kind of exploitable holes there are.

Once you decide to get into a market there are categories, activities that can go on concurrently with other things. What I also want you to notice... so we've got it divided up. We've got research, sales letter, create a product, website and shopping cart, graphics and auto responders.

Let me ask you a question. Why do I have to write the sales letter and wait until the sales letter is done before I have somebody create the graphics? And why do I have to wait until the sales letter is done before I have somebody set up the purchase auto responder and set up the prospect auto responder?

And why do I have to wait until the sales letter is done before I buy the domain name or have the

22

hosting account set up or start working on getting my shopping cart set up or even my ClickBank set up? And why do I have to wait to get the forms set up? And why do I have to wait to get the download page set up? Do you see what I'm getting at here?

The same thing goes while you're brainstorming the headlines, could you be outlining the product? Sure. Now you're not going to do them at the same time. But I want you to see here now that I just had a C pop up next to all of the items that I consider to be "creative." Again, this is going somewhere, because there are really two types of activities that you can engage in. I call them creative or mechanical.

You need to start thinking in terms of what is creative versus what is mechanical. We see here with the C's, things like exploitable holes in the market, brainstorm 50 headlines, 50 bullets. Further we see write the sales letter, polish the sales letter, polish the product, create the product and outline the product. Find and buy the domain name. Thank you confirmation message. Product auto responder mini-course.

Those are all creative things. Those are things when you have to be in a certain state of mind, which is creativity, and we'll talk about when you have that.

Now we also have mechanical activities here. Again, these mechanical points would be more things that are not requiring you to be creative, just things that have to get done. We'll talk about those activities in just a minute. This would be things like the number of sites already out there selling, products already selling online, average price points, and advertising opportunities.

You can see that they're actually very distinct.

The third type of activity is what I would call stuff that should always be outsourced. Unless you are a graphic artist, unless you are somebody who is very proficient at making graphics, I would rather have you create a website and a product that was completely devoid or void or… nah, scratch that.

Don't make a product with any graphics in it if you're going to be the one making the graphics. They're probably suck and they're going to make somebody not want to buy your product. Or if they do

24

they're going to say wow, how amateurish and they're going to return it.

If you're not going to hire a professional to make your graphics, don't make your graphics at all. Don't have any graphics whatsoever.

The big point that I want you to come away from this with, instead of thinking in a linear fashion, thinking of this whole thing as linear, you want to see there are groups of activities that can be accomplished concurrently. And also those activities can be divided into a certain type of activity, either creative or mechanical or those that should be outsourced.

This is all going somewhere. Now I'm about to tell you this is how I get it all done even when my time is totally crunched. My time is more crunched now in a lot of respects, than it was back in 1996 when I really started using this technique to teach myself how to create web pages. Would I do that now if I were starting out? No. Because it cost $150 an hour to have somebody make a website for you. And now you can have an entire website made for about $150.

Would I do it all the same way again? No, not from that respect. But this is the pattern that I came up with to get it done. One of the most frequent questions I get is how are you so prolific, Jim? How do you do 3 or 4 webinars a month? How do you do coaching? How do you do your marketing? How do you come out with new products? How do you do all these things? This is how I do it.

I've come up with a concept that I call the 2 Golden Hours.

The 2 Golden Hours

The 2 Golden Hours basically come down to one creative hour each day and one mechanical hour each day. I do that five days a week. And that's how I hit my goals.

My creative hour is first thing in the morning.

Back in 1996, 1997 my creative hour was from 4:00 in the morning until 5:00 in the morning, unless I was delivering papers. Then it was a little later in the morning because I'd come home and crash and then try to take care of it. The creative hour was first thing in the morning. It was usually from 4:00 to 5:00 or 4:00 to 5:30.

My mechanical hour now is in the afternoon. Now back then it was in the evening because I was going to my job and I had to take care of mechanical stuff when I got home. For me it's in the morning because that's when I'm most creative. Some of my friends are most creative late at night. It's a holdover from college. And the mechanical hour, the time when they can't think, is normally right when they first get up.

For me it's different. When I wake up I'm at my most creative. I'm full of mental energy and I can come up with stuff that I can just... that's when I can do the creative stuff. We're going to talk about which activity should be divided where. But you just need to pay attention to your own self. And with a little bit of careful thought and observation, you can discover when your creative hour is versus when your mechanical hour is. This works for part time and big projects.

I have stuff that I have to get done on a weekly basis, but there are new projects that I want to do. So every time I want to do a new project that goes into my 2 Golden Hours category. It goes into my program for doing the 2 Golden Hours.

If you just do the math, you do 2 hours a day, times 5 days a week, times 4 weeks. That's 40 hours per month devoted solely to whatever project you're working on.

If you are using your workflow effectively and you're working on creative items during the creative time and mechanical items during the mechanical time, the way we divided those things up, then all of a sudden you're able to get stuff done much faster.

You're not trying to do mechanical stuff during your creative time or creative stuff during the mechanical. Then your body and mind are only going to be able to do mechanical stuff, because that's the next thing on the list.

You should never be doing something during one of those timeframes if that's the next thing on the list, unless it falls within that category of either creative or mechanical. You'll see in just a sec.

You notice here that I didn't even include Saturdays. And Saturday, let's say you just worked a half a day, 4 hours on Saturday. That's another 16 hours. That's 56 hours per month that you can devote to a project. Whatever project it is; self-improvement, whatever, getting a website done, whatever the project is, you get 56 focused hours every single month.

Be honest. When you're working on a job do you really work 8 full hours a day? Now most people would say, if you were really honest, no. Because you

29

roll in the morning, you work for about half an hour, 45 minutes, then its break time. Then you do a little bit more work. Then it's time to get ready for lunch so I don't want to start anything. Then you come back from lunch and, man, I'm tired, and so you do a little bit more.

And then it's time for another break. Then you do a little bit more work before the end of the day. But then you don't want to start anything, because quitting time is coming up.

Two to three hours a day is normally the total time where anybody is productive on a job. And the 2 Golden Hours, you're much more likely to be productive. You know why you're doing it and you have a very clear goal in front of you as to what you want to accomplish. And it's for you. It's not building your boss' company; it's not building anybody's life but yours.

What you want to do is understand how to classify action. If you know when your mechanical hour is, when you know when your creative hour is, then you want to take the appropriate actions during that time.

Here are some creative actions in addition to or relisting some of the ones that I showed when we did the Simultaneous Action Channels. They include sales copywriting, writing e-mail teasers, researching and writing articles, designing surveys, brainstorming ideas, keyword research, writing Pay Per Click ads, finding places to advertise, finding link partners, creating outsource bids, designing pop-up offers, researching affiliate offers and evaluating results.

These are things that require you to use your creative bone. Then when you're tired or when you're just not feeling creative, then you can still get things done. You just take care of mechanical actions. That's stuff like posting sales copy to the web.

Writing sales copy requires creativity. Posting sales copy to the web does not require creativity. You have to go through a very definite step-by-step process and there is absolutely no interpretation of it.

Pre-loading auto responders, copying and pasting, that's a mechanical action. Posting and submitting articles, again, that's mostly copy and paste. Posting surveys, that's just uploading stuff. Putting up web-

31

sites, again, uploading files, just making sure the links work.

Keyword list cleaning, that's where you can de-duplicate and fix the words and what not. Placing Pay Per Click ads. Writing Pay Per Click ads requires some good creative thought. But posting them, pasting them into Google's AdWords, for instance, does not require a whole hell of a lot of creativity.

Submitting website ads, finding places and figuring out whether they might be good is very different from actually submitting the ads.

Submitting and trading links ... again, a pretty mindless activity. Placing outsource bids online. Now you want to use some of your creative bone when you figure out what you want somebody to do for you and then post it on RentACoder. But the actual act of putting it on RentACoder, though it requires you not to be in a catatonic trance, doesn't require a whole lot of intelligence to just copy and past and click buttons.

Adding pop-ups to your page or any other type of element to your website, again, doesn't require creativity. Sending broadcast e-mail. Sending an e-

32

mail and making sure it's formatted right is very different from actually writing the e-mail. And things like crunching numbers, compiling statistics and figuring out how things are working on your website. Again, this does not require creativity.

The great thing is when you understand the distinction between the two, you can maximize the time you have available. Instead of trying to get everything done at the... I hesitate to use the word biorhythms, because I think a lot of that is crap, or the way it's been used. But I know from personal experience and from coaching other people, that there are certain times of the day when you can do creative stuff and there are certain times of the day when you should be doing mechanical stuff.

I want to give you a couple more tips on the 2 Golden Hours, this concept.

More Golden Hours Tips

The first is you want to think and pay attention to when you feel most creative versus when you just have spare time but you don't feel creative. Some of you will immediately know, okay, this is when I am. Others of you have probably never even thought about it before. But it's something that you really need to tune into.

I always write my newspaper article on Tuesday morning between the hours of 9:00 AM and 10:30. Now there are other things I have to do, but I have programmed myself to be creative between the hours of 9:00 and 10:30 on Tuesday. I just expect to be creative during that time. You can even train yourself to be creative during certain times.

If you're having trouble finding the time to do 2 hours, cut out 2 hours of TV. Now let me tell you, I used to tell this to everybody, hey, take your TV. If you want to get rich, take your TV, put it out in the middle of the road and hope that it gets run over by a beer truck, because TV keeps you fat, stupid and poor.

I have since changed my tune a little bit because of a nifty little invention called TiVo.   I never really realized how much of television is commercials. Your average hour-long TV show is actually only about 42 minutes. I actually started watching a little bit more television than I used to. I used to "Oh, no TV, jub jah, juba juh."

But now I can watch something and skip through all the commercials and it's really easy. There's some TV that I'm doing.

So if you can't give up the TV, at least get your-self a TiVo, because you can reclaim a lot of time just by taping your favorite shows and watching them when you want to watch them.

But if you cut out 2 hours of TV time you just found the time to do it.

Work a half a day on Saturday if you need to get more done faster. But take at least one day off per week, without exception. No 7-day weeks. Some of you might say, "Oh, Jim, that's easy for you to say because I've heard that you don't have to really work that hard anymore. You've got it made, buddy. Me,

36

I'm just getting started. I need to make money now, buddy."

Okay. Well, here's the problem, genius. If you work 7 days a week you will be about as creative as somebody who's been hit in the head with a rock, because your mind needs time to relax. Your mind needs time to unwind. Your mind needs time to recover. If you work yourself 7 days a week, like "Oh, I'm making it happen. I'm achieving." The problem is you won't be creative, so the time when you're working will be terribly inefficient.

You would be better off working 5-1/2 days a week focused, really hitting it hard. Then try resting and recuperating rather than trying to be one of these people who makes it happen 7 days a week. And I am talking from direct, personal experience, because I went for almost 3 years working 7 days a week. And it turned me into a wreck.

Now, next thing you want to do is make sure you schedule the 2 hours in your calendar every single day, just like you would any other appointment. You would never think about missing a client appointment or an appointment with your boss or an appointment

37

with other important people in your life. So this is going to be the method you're going to use to have your project that's going to get you the freedom that you're looking for. Why on earth would you not treat that with the same respect that you would an appointment with somebody like your insurance agent?

In fact, the appointments that you have with yourself for those 2 hours every single day should be the most important appointments of the day. And when you really know when your most creative hour is, you would never devote that hour to anything other than the most important project in your life and in your business.

The bottom line is, get up an hour earlier if you must. Now I know, "I need to sleep, Jim." Okay, go to bed an hour earlier and get up an hour sooner. Again, the reason most people stay up late at night, unless you're making whoopee, is watching television. Cut out the TV, go to bed an hour earlier, and get up an hour earlier.

Especially if you have kids, get up an hour before the kids get up. If you've got to get the kids off to school, then you need to be up an hour before they are. "Oh, Jim, you don't understand. I mean, I've got stuff

38

to do." Okay, you either take action or you make an excuse. You bite the bullet and you make it happen. Suck it up and drive on.

Okay, now that we've gotten through the sympathy hour, let's talk for a minute. Now that we know how to take action, we need to know what we want to take action on. Now those who fail to plan, plan to fail. And we're going to talk about how to prioritize which projects you want to work on first.

2 Types of Planning

From my experience, one of the biggest mistakes, if not the biggest mistake, is trying to get too much done or trying to get too many projects done all at once. So you either try to get too much done at once or too many projects rolling and you never finish anything. Proper planning and execution are really key at this point.

There are two types of planning that we all have to go through when we're trying to get a result.

The first type of planning is strategic planning. This is like Army generals looking at little men or little tanks or little planes on a great big board and they see where things are going.

With strategic planning you see where you're going. There's lots of information out there on the market about this. It's basically where you're going and why you're going there. So a lot of this is things like yearly goal setting or your personal purpose statement or any big picture stuff.

Again, this is the vast majority of stuff out there on the market.   You look at what's out there as far as books and tapes and programs. People are teaching you how to set goals and how to have a purpose and all this other stuff, but there's really no measurable result from this.   They're hoping, and I'm just going to say it, because I've got a lot of stuff to get through here. If you ever want to debate this, if we ever meet, you can drink a beer and I'll drink an O'Doul's and we can discuss this.

My personal opinion, the vast majority of strategic planning information, goal setting stuff and all that out there is complete and total crap. It's all rehashed.   It's people teaching what they learned from other people. They're trying to put a spin on it in order to get people to buy their book which will teach you the right habits or the right this or the right that. And when you try and sit down and apply it, it's total crap and it doesn't work. There, I said it. My webinar.

Two types of planning.   The second type of planning is tactical planning. And this is also known as action planning. This is where you get down to what needs to get done today, tomorrow, etc. This is where you make a list. And then you've got to decide, and I

42

said this earlier, who's going to do it? Either you do it or other people or systems do it for you. And you've also got to decide when it's going to get done.

There's not a whole heck of a lot out there in the world on tactical planning or proper tactical planning in your business, action planning in your life and business. And this is where everybody fails miserably, in the tactical planning. The reason when you get right down to it, 99% of all the training out there consists of, "take out a legal pad, write down your to-do list and then prioritize it."

Somebody might sell you a real fancy checklist to use this for and a whole bunch of letters and check-marks and X's and other things to help you know whether you got through your to-do list or not. But the problem is that we've never been properly trained to evaluate and prioritize. That means most people end up working on the urgent instead of the important.

What's important is the stuff that's going to have the biggest impact on your life. But what's urgent is usually the stuff that's a pain in the, you know what, stuff you just want to get rid of right then. But the urgent is usually the least valuable to your business. So

43

we need a system, and I have one that I'm about to share with you, that enables you to quickly evaluate all the available choices for taking action. Then it's going to help you figure out which actions to take that are going to give you the most impact for the least amount of effort.

Really, tactics are where the rubber meets the road and this is where stuff gets done. So you need to understand how to engage in effective action planning.

Here's the solution. And it's my Fast Action Matrix.

The Fast Action Matrix

This is actually based on the exact system used by US Special Forces, that would be Navy Seals and Green Berets, to evaluate which terrorists and other enemy targets to eliminate and in what order. Basically the Fast Action Matrix is my adaptation, it's my system for thoroughly evaluating and prioritizing all available projects, activities, and ideas.

I have something that's going to be available for you when we have the download of the replay of this webinar. It's 3 pages. Now listen very, very closely to me.

You have my permission to take these pages, print off as many copies as you need to use for your own personal use whenever you need to use them. Or you may print one copy and make as many photocopies as you need to make for your own personal use.

You may not share this with anyone else. You may not sell this to anyone else. You may not use this for anyone else. This is for you.

The first page, basically, gets you all pumped up about it and it tells you what it is. Then it has you write down... we're going to go through this in just a sec. I'm just giving you an overview. It has you write down your overall purpose or mission for your life or your business right now. And then it takes you through a scoring system, where you're going to score, based on various categories which we're going to go through here in just a sec.

The Entrepreneurial
Prioritization Matrix

"Learn to use the same techniques the Navy Seals & Army "Green Berets" use to prioritize the destruction of enemy terrorist targets... and how to apply those same techniques in the entrepreneurial arena for maximum return in your business!"

- **Reduce Stress by knowing exactly where to focus your available time (no matter how busy or stressed out you think you are)...**

- **Increase Income through the power of focused effort (instead of acting like the "poor" who mismanage their time)...**

- **Maximize existing resources to get more from what you've already got (often, the key is not more or better tools, it's using what you have more effectively)...**

Short-Term, Intermediate-Term Goal / Idea / Evaluation and Prioritization Exercise

Part 1 - Clearly state the overall purpose or "mission" for your life right now:

_____

_____

_____

Part 2 – Based on the overall purpose or mission for your life right now, evaluate each of the ideas / potential courses of action based on the following questions:

Evaluate each on a scale of 1 to 5

1 = Least Valuable / Very Hard / Most Difficult
5 = Most Valuable / Very Easy / Least Difficult

(1) Based on my mission, how vital is it for my life / my business to get this done?
   1 = Not critical   2 = Slightly critical 3 = Fairly critical
   4 = Very critical   5 = Extremely critical

(2) How easily can I clarify the steps needed to get this done?
   1 = Not very easily 2 = Slightly easily   3 = Fairly easily
   4 = Very easily   5 = Extremely easily

(3) How easily can I take the actions / delegate the actions necessary to get this done?

1 = Not very easily 2 = Slightly easily   3 = Fairly easily
4 = Very easily   5 = Extremely easily

(4) Based on my existing resources, how much EFFORT am I going to have to expend in order to accomplish this goal or manifest this idea?
1 = EXTREME EFFORT 2 = Significant Effort   3 = Fair amount of effort 4 = Not much effort 5 = "Cake Walk!"

(5) What's the overall / relative value to my life and business of getting this done?
1 = Not very valuable   2 = Slightly valuable 3 = Fairly valuable 4 = Very valuable 5 = Extremely valuable

(6) How happy will getting this done make me?
1 = Totally indifferent 2 = Slightly happy 3 = Fairly happy
4 = Very happy   5 = Jumping out of my skin in ecstasy

Download the complete printable Matrix at:
www.TrueLifeSuccessLessons.com/matrix

Target Goal Evaluation Matrix

Goal / Idea	1. How Vital?	2. Clarify Steps?	3. Ease Action?	4. Amount of Effort?	5. Overall Value?	6. Happy Finish?	Total / Rank	Comments
1							/	
2							/	
3							/	
4							/	
5							/	
6							/	
7							/	
8							/	
9							/	
10							/	

49

So literally what you do is list them all off here on the left of the sheet. If you need to print off more than one, go ahead.

Download the complete printable Matrix at: www.TrueLifeSuccessLessons.com/matrix

Then you're going to rank them based on the criteria that we're going to go through here. This is going to help you, whether you're trying to figure out which project you should do first, or figure out which aspect of a certain project you should do first. On virtually anything, this will help you decide, based on criteria that we're going to go over here in just a sec.

Any projects or to-do's that you could spend time on, you use this so that you know which ones will get you to your objectives first. Again, I'm going to have that page I just showed you. That will be available on the download page or from the replay page for this webinar. So no worries there, you'll be able to get your hands on this. If you're live with me you'll have it in your hands in less than 24 hours. If you are watching the replay, it's available further on down the screen.

Basically, the Fast Action Matrix, again, is based on something that Special Forces use. It's called the CARVER Method. I'm not going to get into what all of those initials stand for. But basically C stands for criticality; A for accessibility; R for recuperability' V for vulnerability; E for effect and R for recognizability. In and of itself, it's kind of hard to use. But I converted it over to something that makes a lot more sense when you're trying to prioritize. That's where the Fast Action Matrix came from.

The first question you want to ask is how vital is it to me. So when you're looking at each one of those items that you're trying to prioritize, how vital is it to me? How easily can I clarify the steps to take? How easy is it to take action? How many of the resources that I need are already available to me? What's the overall value? And what's the overall effect on my happiness?

How do we use it? The first step is to clearly write down and define your short term or medium term purpose or mission in your life right now, where you're going. Because if you don't know where you're going and why, then you're not going to know where you want to end up. It may sound simple, but I can tell you, when I ask people, okay, why are we doing this?

"Well, I want to make some money" or "I'm tired of working for my job." Not a good enough reason.

It can be a goal for your business, it can be a specific dollar figure that you want. It can basically be anything else that you're moving towards. This answers the question of what's the point of all this once you get started, especially if you're doing a project that may be bigger or harder or more difficult or arduous. If you know why you're doing it, if you know where you want to end up and you know why you want to end up there as it relates to your life, then you're much more likely to have the endurance power to stick with it.

So how do we use the Fast Action Matrix? Well, again, let's look at a couple of examples of Mission Statements. This is an example, this is a general example. "My Mission is to provide maximum value for my customers and subscribers by enriching and empowering them, while maximizing profit in the shortest period of time possible."

In this one I'm probably going to be evaluating, if this is the Mission Statement. I'm going to be evaluating various courses of action as far as what type of project I should do or which project idea I should be going after.

A medium example would be "I want to have my new product completed as soon as possible." Now if this is my current Mission Statement, probably what I'm going to be doing is listing off various action items that have to take place in order to get this product done. So it would probably be a lot of items that would be similar to the examples that I was using earlier about getting your website up or getting all the various activities done.

Another example would be "My mission is to net $20,000 or more in the shortest period of time." Again, this is probably going to be used to evaluate various options of different projects that I could be doing, as opposed to specific things to do within those projects at that point.

The other thing I want to point out to you, I'm going to talk more about this in a minute. On here you notice I say, "$20,000 or more in the shortest period of time." Notice I didn't say, "Okay, $20,000 within 30 days." And there's a definite reason why I think it's idiotic to state your goal or to state an intention in that

53

way, when it comes to having a deadline on your actual goal achievement or on your actual outcome. I'm going to discuss that with you in just a minute, but I want to tease you a little bit right there.

We've got our mission statement. Now the next thing we do in the Matrix, in this right here, in this Prioritization Matrix, Fast Action Matrix. We list off all the current things to do on your plate. The things you want to get done, the goals you want to accomplish, ideas you want to act on, courses of action you could take, tasks you want to complete. Basically it's all the miscellaneous stuff you feel like you need to get done.

You know, the stuff that wakes you up in the middle of the night. The stuff that will get you up early. It will have you worrying in your bed about how you're going to get it all done or what you should do next, or feeling overwhelmed. You list all that stuff off here. Like I said, you may have to print off two or three or four copies of this one, so that you can list off everything you need to get done.

Next thing you do, keeping in mind your current purpose or mission on a scale of 1 to 5, you're then going to score each item based on the 6 evaluation criteria. We're going to run through this and I'm going to give you some examples. This will make perfect sense to you.

A score of 1 would be an item that's least valuable or very hard to do or most difficult to achieve. And a score of 5 would be something that was most valuable or very easy or least difficult to achieve.

Criteria 1 is how vital is it for my life and my business to get this done. One would be not critical and 5 would be extremely critical and we've got all the points in between. But if something's not critical for your life to get it done or critical for your business, you can use those two interchangeably, depending on what the purpose is that you're evaluating right now.

If it's not really vital for your life or for your business, that's strike 1. But if it's really critical, then you need to acknowledge that. Again, we're getting back to the difference between urgent versus important.

Criteria No. 2. "How easily can I clarify the steps needed to get this done?" 1, not very easily, 5 extremely easily. Again, it might be important, but if you can't figure out how to get it done then it might not

55

be something that you want to concentrate on. This would include a business project, as opposed to something where, all things being equal, something that you can't figure out what to do, versus something where you can figure out how to do it.

Criteria No. 3 is "How easily can I take the actions, delegate the actions necessary to get this done?" Again, it needs to get done. How easily can you do it or how easily can you delegate to someone else to do it?

Again, let's use the example of graphics. I suck at making graphics. If this said how easily can I take the actions necessary to get this done when it came down to getting the graphics done for my website, for example. The answer would have to be No. 1. But since I know where to go to outsource the graphics, and it's really easy, all of a sudden that becomes a 5.

Also, the way we phrase this forces you to think not just about how you can do it, but how you can delegate it.

Again, I used to think in terms of how I can do it or how I'm the one that has to do it. But remember,

56

knowing what needs to get done doesn't mean that you're the one that has to do it. So how easily can I take the actions, versus delegate the actions necessary to get this done.

Criteria No. 4. "Based on my existing resources," and this is key. It would be easy for me to take a trip to the moon if I had a rocket, a trained crew, a $2 billion budget and all the time in the world. But I don't have that, so it would be

damn hard for me to go to the moon. "Based on my existing resources how much effort am I going to have to expend in order to accomplish this goal or manifest this idea?" One would be extreme effort and 5 would be a cakewalk.

Criteria No. 5 is "What's the overall relative value to my life and business of getting this done?" One would be not very valuable and 5 would be extremely valuable.

Finally, No. 6, "How happy will getting this done make me?" Think about it for a second. One of the things that I have realized, and I did realize when I was lying in a hospital bed. The top of my heart was going at 178 beats a minute, the bottom part of my heart couldn't keep up. I had blood pooling in the chambers of my heart. And was told there was a real danger of my developing a clot that would cause me to have a stroke. I realized that business though important, ultimately in the end all we have is the happiness that we feel and the love that we feel for others.

I'm not trying to get all '60's and waving flowers at you. But all things being equal, you had two projects where they were identical based on the first 5 criteria that we went through. But one of them left you totally indifferent and not really giving a rat's patoot, and the other one had you jumping out of your skin with ecstasy, then that's the one you should do.

But unless you evaluate it with this criteria, a lot of times you end up doing things that you think other people would think that you should do. Or, you think this is what most people would do or whatever. But ultimately, you always have to do stuff that's going to make you happy.

Once you've gone through these 6 criteria, all you do is come over here and total these up. You just add them up all the way over here, each one. Then you total up the points for each target, and the highest score

58

is the first one that you attack. Then you start with that one and work it until you can't work it anymore. And then you move on to the next one.

Again, if it's projects, you should be finishing that project, or if something happens and you can't finish, then you move on to the next one.

If you're planning activities within a project, let's say you're launching your website and you're going through all those steps we went through before. Then you run into a point where you can't do something, then at least you're not stopped and the whole project comes to a screeching halt. You move on to the next thing that you can work on while you figure out how to solve the little roadblock that you got.

A lot of times when you keep on moving, that roadblock stopping you before has a way of just solving itself. Objects in motion tend to stay in motion as opposed to people that stop, sit down in the middle of the road and cry like a damn baby. "Oh, it's not working out. This doesn't work. Jim's full of it. I can't do an online business, because I don't know how to put up a website."

Okay, well there's other stuff you can work on.

Now let's look at a couple of real life examples from my business activities where I've actually used this process. And I've used this process within the last week. This is not what I used it on, but this is an example of how I've used it.

Real Life Examples

Things recently demanding my time and attention. "I need to modify the www.eBookfire.com affiliate program so people can advertise on Google AdWords." People keep asking me for that every single week.

"Revamp the sales letter for a product re-release. Release Affiliate Cloaker 4.0. And get a new affiliate toolbox done for www.eBookfire.com."

The first one is "Modify affiliate programs so people can advertise on Google AdWords." So how vital is it? I scored that a 4. Clarify steps, 4. Ease of action, 3. Amount of effort, 3. Total value, 3. Happy when finished, 3.

I was kind of neutral about the whole thing. You know, sales are still coming in and I don't think it's going to really raise sales that much, so it was a middle of the road. It wasn't doing a whole lot for me.

Next one on the list. "Sales letter for product re-release." How vital was it? It was damn vital, because I had the project just sitting there. I needed to convert the sales letter over from being an eClass over to a home study course. How easily could I clarify the steps, a 5. I just needed to rewrite the sales letter so that it was selling a product instead of selling an eClass.

Ease of action, it was a 4. I mean, it was like a 35 page sales letter, so there was some effort there, but it was still pretty easy. Amount of effort was a 4. It was just sitting down, gutting it out and doing it. Total value was a 5, because as soon as I got the sales letter up I knew I'd be making money. And happy when finished, I knew the thing was going to sell.

"Release Affiliate Cloaker 4.0." How vital was it? It was a 4. I mean, there's some stuff on there, there are new features on that where I think people would get a lot of value. Clarify the steps, 4. Pretty easy to do. Ease of action, there's some things I'm going to have to do, including redoing the Help Manual. Amount of effort was a 3. Total value was a 3. Happy when finished was a 4.

"Get new affiliate toolbox done for www.eBookfire.com" How vital, 5. I mean, I've got… my affiliates are a big part of my business. Clarify the

62

steps, easy. Ease of action, 4, because I know I'm not going to be the one doing it. Amount of effort was a 4. Total value 4. Happy when finished 4.

Then I just went through and added them all up. So here are all the things I needed to get done. And so the www.eBookfire.com, so people could do Google AdWords was a 20. Sales letter for a mini-site creator re-release was a 28. Release Affiliate Link Cloaker 4.0 was a 21. And get new affiliate toolbox done for www.eBookfire.com.

This is the one that got done first. And this is the one that got done second. And actually, I'm having it redone again to reflect a whole bunch of changes. And I just got the deal inked on that today. So we'll have a new toolbox within the next 30 days.

Here are the results that I got. Got the sales letter redone in 2 days. I just gutted it out and got it done. Yeah, I did spend more than 2 hours a day on it, but I could. And I generated over $800,000 in sales in less than 12 months. I delegated the affiliate toolbox to my programmer. Decided to shelve the Affiliate Link Cloaker launch. I still haven't released it. The product still sells. People are happy with it. And I wondered why in the heck I was so stressed out.

The point of all this is when should you use the Fast Action Matrix? Well, whenever you're pressed for time and you have to devote your time to the absolutely most critical task to accomplish your mission or your purpose. And guys, if you're wondering "Jim, do you really print that out and use it?" Yes. I really do print it out. I really do get a real pen in my hand. And I write down all the crap that's driving me nuts, the stuff where I'm trying to figure what I should do first. I prioritize it and I get it straight and I just get it done.

I really do use it, and I use it often. So anytime you don't know where to start first, "Man, I just don't know where to get started." Well, here's the solution. And anytime you're feeling overwhelmed with all the stuff you have to get done, you break out this thing, you print it off, you list it all out. You evaluate it intelligently the way I've shown you, and then you prioritize it intelligently. And you know that when you're doing your 2 Golden Hours a day, you're working on the absolute most important thing that you should be working on right now, based on your position and direction in life at this moment.

64

Deadlines VS. Goals

Now, an important note about deadlines versus goals. I told you earlier, remember, I took umbrage when everybody says okay, "I want $100,000 by December 31, 2015." And your brain says, you've never made $100,000 before in your life. How in the hell are you going to make $100,000 between now and the end of the month, or now and the end of the year, which is like 3 months away? Hell, no, that's not going to work. Screw that, let's go watch TV.

You never take effective action because your mind doesn't believe that it's going to actually happen.

You need to understand that you can put a deadline on action that you or someone is going to take. You can say I'm going to have the first draft of my sales letter done by September 30th. Or I'm going to make sure that the graphics are done by October 1st at 5:00 o'clock PM. That's the deadline. And that's when they need to be delivered.

I can say okay, by October 3rd I'm going to write out the first 4 auto responder messages for my mini-course. Any action can have a deadline on it. But you cannot put a deadline on the achievement of a goal.

I want $200,000 by next Monday. I mean, I can say that. And even in my gut I think, how in the hell am I going to get in 3 days how am I going to raise $200,000. But I can say I want to make $200,000 as fast as possible. Let me brainstorm some ways I can make it happen. And then I'm going to prioritize those projects to see which one can get me closest to that the fastest.

But if I say $200,000 by next Monday, the brain shuts down. The brain is going to tell you... it's not even going to believe it. Here's the other thing, it won't believe you or your brain will go "Oh, I've got plenty of time. I want to make $100,000 by December 31st, 2008. Oh, hell, that's 15 months. I'll worry about that next summer." That's literally what your subconscious is doing.

But if you say I want $200,000 as fast as possible, that's a better way to state it. The key to all this is to break down all the action steps to your goal. And I prefer to do it in those simultaneous workflows, that No. 2 that I showed you. And then put a deadline on each action step and you will reach your goal. You have to.

By having deadlines placed on actions, that's how you know whether you're getting closer to or further away from the outcome that you're looking for. But again, you cannot put a deadline on an outcome. But you can sure as heck put a deadline on specific actions.

The bottom line with all this, effective action planning is the key to your success. And if I had to make a little correction to this or an addition, it would be effective action planning and execution are the keys to your success. Because it's knowing what you've got to do and then doing it, either you doing it or somebody else doing it, and planning out each action down to a specific date.

Live Reader Questions

Now we do have some specific questions that were submitted ahead of time, as well as some live Q&A. I'm interested to see what you think of this, whether you guys are sitting out there yawning and booing or going" dang, I picked up some stuff. This is pretty interesting".

I would like to know, just to kind of help me, how likely are you to take advantage of the information from this Webinar. Are you very likely, likely, not likely, no way, not my thing? Let me know whether this is something you think you might act on or not. So how likely are you to take advantage of the information from this Webinar, very likely, likely, not likely, no way, not my thing.

We've got 64% of the votes in. We're up to 67. Come on, guys, vote, and we can get to the live portion of tonight's presentation. Always good. I promise that I still have my pants on at this point.

Five, four, three, two, one. All right. Let's take a look at the results. 79% of you are very likely to take advantage of this information, and 21% are likely. And nobody said not likely or no way, not my thing. So good, that means you at least picked up some stuff that you think you could act on.

Question:

Now, move on to subscriber submitted questions. The first one is from Judy. Judy says "The biggest thing stopping me many days is my having a question to ask, usually a technical one, and not having anyone to ask. So a project that could potentially make me a lot of money goes undone while I go back to working on my bricks and mortar business, which I know inside and out. Very depressing."

Okay, Judy, couple of things. No. 1, you can… if you have a question, especially a technical question that you don't know how to answer. You don't know the answer, one of the things that you can do is go to www.rentacoder.com and just pay someone to answer your question. The funny thing, especially if it's a technical question. A lot of times if you post the question and say okay, I will pay you, I'll pay for the answer to this. A lot of times, especially… one man's mystery is another person's old news.

A lot of times you will have somebody just answer the question for you and they won't even charge you. They'll just say okay, here's the answer to your question. Pay me whatever you think it's worth.

Another place that you can go is www.answers.google.com. Now, www.answers.google.com is not taking new questions anymore. It was a place where you could go, you could post a question and then people would bid on answering your question. Or you could say how much… I forget, maybe it was you said how much you'd pay. They folded it up because it didn't work out quite how they thought it would. But the thing is, the database is still there last time I looked, which was last week.

You can go to www.answers.google.com, you can do a search on what's troubling you. You may have found that somebody else asked the same question and paid somebody to answer it, and you can get the answer for nothing.

The other thing to remember, Judy, what I'm seeing here is somebody, I could be wrong, but I'm inferring from this that you're working in a linear way. And now we know that we can do simultaneous

71

workflow paths. Hell, it says simultaneous, don't worry about whether it's spelled right or not. The point is, though, that if you get stuck in one area, you have other areas that you can move to. Then you either hire somebody to figure out the issue or hire somebody to just do it for you in the place that's holding you back.

I think that those three things will help you overcome a lot of obstacles.

Question:
Next one. "I know you have personal Golden Hours to get things done, 4:00 AM, I believe, but how does that affect you later on in the day? Do you hit a wall and crash out or do you have a mega Jimbo tonic that keeps you going?"

It's interesting, because I used to survive on caffeine and cigarettes, and we saw where that ended me, or got me with everything. But when I'm in that mode where I want to work at 4:00 o'clock in the morning, I don't stay up late. I go to bed at 8:30 or 9:00 o'clock at night. If you've got kids, then make their little butts go to bed at 8:30 or 9:00 o'clock at night.

Normally what I'm doing now, or lately, I'm going to bed at 10:00 at night and I'm getting up at 5:30. Normally I'm at work at 6:00. So my creative time now, I can do this full time, I'm working from… my creative hours are from 6:00 to 9:00 or from 6:00 to 10:30. That's when I'm doing creative stuff.

After then it's really hard for me to do more creative stuff. This is when I'm doing my writing, my articles, planning stuff, creating PowerPoint's, doing whatever. But the key here, if you're going to get up early, go to bed at a reasonable time. I don't take naps anymore, because I'm not staying up too late. That's the answer to it. If I go to bed at 11:00 or 12:00 o'clock at night, I don't get up until 6:30 or 7:330.

I mean, I've just found that if I make sure that I get my 7 or 8 hours of sleep, then for me the first couple of hours, couple, 3 hours when I get up are my most creative time. So there's no magic to it other than getting enough sleep.

The other thing, if you really want to super-charge this and get yourself to the point where you don't need as much sleep, go exercise. Don't be like Jim. Don't sit on your fat ass all week and then be a weekend warrior running around the paintball field and getting out of breath after 2 minutes. Walk 3 times a week. Get some exercise, and that will help you, too. I'm yelling at myself in a public forum.

Again, I'll come back to this, if you're having trouble finding the time, if you've got kids, you've got a spouse, you've got a family, got responsibility, great. The kids don't eat from 6:00 at night until 9:00 or 10:00 o'clock at night. Cut out TV. I guarantee you this will solve at least an hour of your problem a day.

Don't watch the nightly news. It sucks. There's nothing good on there. They're just playing the crap to get you to hang from one cliffhanger to the next so that you'll watch the ads. There's nothing good on nightly news. You can skip that. There, I just found you a half a magic Golden Hour.

Question:
"What are the 3 best… what are your 3 best stay on track techniques?" Well, the No. 1 is to operate from a checklist every single day. Once I know what I want to get done, once I know why I'm doing it, once I know where it fits in the priorities of my life. I've done all that stuff and I'm in the actual doing it, doing it,

doing it mode. I have a little, I guess it's 7x10 or maybe it's 6x8, I don't know, a little pad, a little steno pad. Every day I write the date at the top, I list off all the stuff I want to get done and as I get it done I write an X next to it.

As far as the staying on track, we already went over them. Knowing what I want to get done and why I want to get it done and where it fits, where everything I'm doing fits in my master plan. That helps keep me on focus and it helps keep me on point and moving forward and staying on track. Having a checklist and knowing what I want to do, why I want to do it and where it fits in my master plan.

"Imagine you're one of us disorganized guys with a ton of diverse tasks to prioritize. Just what are your thought processes when tackling such a problem?" I would say you want to use the Matrix that I gave you. John, that's the answer. That's why… and you know, there's not a… it's not that you're disorganized or you're organized. It's just what strategies are you employing.

I still in a lot of respects consider myself very disorganized. Though I have a lot of people tell me,

75

man, you're one of the most organized people I know. But it's because I focus on what's important and what's going to get me where I want to go the fastest. And I pretty much ignore everything else. I will say if I'm blessed with anything, it's tunnel vision.

Question:

"How do you get quickly past any sticking points that hold up the process? Sometimes my 2-hour project is missing something, that is in its own right, a 2- to 4-hour project."

Again, by understanding, (a) my creative hour versus my mechanical hour. Then understanding that there are multiple things that need to get done that can get done in order to get the whole project closer to fruition. If I get stuck on one, I move on to the next. Then while figuring out how to solve this problem, the whole thing doesn't grind to a halt. I'm still moving forward and still making progress. Again, objects and motions tend to stay in motion.

As you're doing these other things, I'm not going to get into the whole metaphysical workings of the universe. But normally when your intention is clear, when you know exactly what you want, why you want it and you're moving towards it, the answers have a way of appearing. Or maybe not the answer to this question that's holding you up. But you find a way to get around it so that you don't even have to solve the problem, you're just able to move on down the trail.

You go over it, around it, behind it, under it, however. Anyway, that's what I do there.

LIVE Questions:
Now it's time to see if we have any live Q&A. Let's look in our Q&A box and see if we have any questions.

Suzanne says "Even better, rather than using it only when you're feeling stressed and don't know what to do first, be more proactive rather than reactive and use it to prevent getting stressed out." Very good point. Great point, Suzanne.

"In the Fast Action Matrix are you evaluating both creative and mechanical functions?" No, I'm not making any distinction. What I'm doing is figuring out what needs to get done. Once I know what needs to get done I can prioritize that and then do the creative things

77

during the creative hour. I can do the mechanical stuff during the mechanical hour.

In the Fast Action Matrix, I don't make any distinction as to whether or not it's going to be a creative thing or whatever. I'm just looking at the activity or the idea or the project or whatever it is. I'm looking at it from the standpoint of how fast can I get it done; how easily can I get it done; how much effort, etc. etc.

Once you figure out what needs to get done, then you start just implementing it on a day-to-day basis.

That was it for the questions. Lets draw this to a conclusion.

I'll be very curious to hear what you guys think about this, because I've taught the 2 Golden Hours before and some of this before to an extent. But the ways of getting this done and the action channels, linear versus simultaneous, I've never taught that before. A lot of thought went into that. I'll be curious to see whether you liked it or not.

Conclusion

What we covered today, two paths for getting any project done. How I get it all done, even when my time is crunched.

I don't know if I mentioned it or not, but even with all the stuff I've got going on, it's easy... Frankly, the easiest online business you're ever going to start is the first one, because you have absolutely no distractions. Once you get a bunch of stuff going on it's easy to feel like you're working, that you're doing stuff. But in order to move forward, there always has to be progress. This is the way that I always keep progress moving.

No matter how busy I am, I know that I can find the 2 hours to get the next thing rolling on down the trail.

We talked about how to prioritize, which projects to work on first. Two types of planning, strategic versus action. We went over the Fast Action Matrix. Talked about deadlines versus goals. We went over previously submitted questions. Live Q&A about this session's topics. And much, much more.

I have some final thoughts for you. Start where you are with what you have right now. Some people might think that that's a trite phrase. And that's just "Oh, you even pulled that out of a Nightingale Conan program." I don't know where in the heck I heard that first.

Start where you are with what you have right now. So many people are waiting to get started. They're waiting for something outside of themselves to finally make sure everything is perfect, everything is right, everything is exactly the way it's supposed to be. I've got news for you, it's time to wake up. It's never going to happen.

There's never going to be a perfect time to do anything. You're going to be tired, you're going to be busy. Aunt Tilly's going to be sick. The dog might have the mange. Whatever it is, there's always some-thing in the way if you're waiting for a perfect set of circumstances to arise. It's never going to happen.

Stop waiting to get started. Adopt the, "do it now", mantra in your life. That's one of the biggest things that I have done. If something needs doing, do it now. Do it now, do it now. Try organizing it into these 2 Golden Hours, by learning how to segment the different types of work and having it prioritized. Then you can be like the builder who gets the bigger house done in less than half the time of the knucklehead builder, who's doing it all step-by-step-by-step in a linear fashion.

Finally, take action on your goal for 2 hours every day no matter what. You will get it to the point where you can't live without it. That's the only way that you will really feel productive, like you've accomplished anything, if you get your 2 focused Golden Hours in for the day.

Once you get to that point, once you know that you really have worked on something and you've given it an honest effort, that is when all the power of the universe gets behind you and your goal is all but achieved already. All you need to do is just keep following through.

I'm Jim Edwards. I want to thank you very much. Those of you that are live with me tonight, I would really appreciate your feedback, please, on the evaluation form that should pop up when the webinar is over.

We'll look forward to seeing you soon.

MORE HELP FROM JIM EDWARDS

Find out more about Jim's latest projects here:

BULK BOOK ORDER &

CUSTOMIZED VERSION INFORMATION

Most **AQuickReadBook.com** titles are available at special quantity discounts for bulk purchases for sales promotions, premiums, fundraising, gifts or educational use.

In other words, if you'd like to get a truckload of copies of this book (or even just a dozen or two) to hand out at an event, company function, or as gifts to your clients, we can help you out at a substantial discount over the cover price.

Just contact us and we'll get you a quote. ☺

Also, special customized / company specific versions or excerpts can be created to fit specific needs. So if you'd like to do something customized with this book, drop us a line and we'll discuss it with you.

Our goal is to help you get what you need and to help our authors help as many people as possible with their books.

For more information, please contact us at A Quick Read Book™ online at www.AQuickReadBook.com

www.ingramcontent.com/pod-product-compliance
Lightning Source LLC
Chambersburg PA
CBHW071238170526
45165CB00003B/1151